Let's Draw a C***K on It

JOHN THOMAS

Let's Draw a C**K on It

JOHN THOMAS

THE MEMBERS-ONLY DOODLE BOOK

Michael O'Mara Books Limited

First published in Great Britain in 2013 by
Michael O'Mara Books Limited
9 Lion Yard
Tremadoc Road
London SW4 7NQ

Copyright © Michael O'Mara Books Limited 2013

A CIP catalogue record for this book is available from the British Library.

Papers used by Michael O'Mara Books Limited are natural, recyclable products made from wood grown in sustainable forests. The manufacturing processes conform to the environmental regulations of the country of origin.

ISBN: 978-1-78243-150-3 in hardback print format

1 2 3 4 5 6 7 8 9 10

www.mombooks.com

Picture credits: 'Aim high': KenHT/Shutterstock; 'Penis Museum': Elín Eydís Friðriksdóttir; 'Nether regions' (right): Jcmurphy/Wikimedia Commons; 'What about Little Elvis?': George Rose/Getty Images; 'Take a load of that': Vincenzo Pinto/AFP/Getty Images; 'Penis park': Amanderson/Wikimedia Commons; 'Penis theft': Per-Anders Pettersson/Getty Images; 'Tittle my cock': Malleus Fatuorum/Wikipedia Commons; 'Hello, sailor': Brian Burton Arsenault/Shutterstock.com; 'One we made earlier . . .': Matt Cardy/Getty Images

All other images www.shutterstock.com, except 'Big grass boner', 'Nether regions' (left), 'Pissing contest' and 'Spit it out'

Cover design by Greg Stevenson
Designed and typeset by Greg Stevenson

Printed and bound in China

Introduction

Measuring an impressive eleven metres from the tip of the cock to the bottom of the ball sack, the Cerne Abbas Giant, carved in chalk on the Downs in the county of Dorset, has the largest genitals in the UK. Over the years there has been much academic speculation from boffins all round the world about what the figure represents and why it has such a mighty wanger. Some say it is a Saxon deity, others that it is actually a portrait of the Roman hero Hercules.

However, the eggheads seemed to have missed the most obvious explanation – that a group of ancient schoolboys carved the jumbo stiffy on their last day of term. It wouldn't surprise me at all if the giant also bore a passing resemblance to their headmaster.

Of course these youthful pranksters weren't the first people to take pleasure in the drawing of cock and balls. Recently discovered cave art in France, which experts date as being over 10,000 years old, shows tiny grinning* stick people with erect spurting penises, running around among the more familiar images of woolly mammoths and bison.

So please do not think that when you are adding a flaccid member or a hairy pair of balls

to the photographs within these pages you are doing something puerile and childish – in fact you are continuing an age-old and venerable tradition.

Let's draw a cock on it . . .

JOHN THOMAS
Cockermouth, England

*the stick people weren't actually grinning,
I made that up.

Believe it, baby

Nothing for ages, then
they all come at once

As you like it

Keep it under your hat

Big grass boner

· ·

In May 2009, pranksters in New Zealand climbed into the grounds of a local college and sketched out six cocks of varying sizes on the grass. The principal said that the penises started appearing a few days later, but that by then there was 'not really much we could do about it; the caretaker took some more weedkiller and tried to camouflage it a bit.'

Then a local man spotted them on Google Earth; the story went viral and was reported the world over. And while the grassy cocks have in reality disappeared, they still exist virtually on Google for us all to appreciate. Thank God for the Internet (and weedkiller).

Ye Olde Worlde Cock 'n' Balls

Old boy
. . . .

OMG
· · · · · · · · · · · ·

Threesome
· · · · · · · · · · ·

Puerile eruptions

In AD 79 the Italian volcano Mount Vesuvius erupted, covering the surrounding area in lava and burying the towns of Pompeii and Herculaneum. They lay undiscovered, frozen in time, for 1,500 years.

When work was begun to dig them up, it wasn't just buildings that were revealed but also a large amount of ancient graffiti. It is reassuring to know that the Romans were as keen on writing rude things on walls as we are. Here are some of the best:

WEEP, YOU GIRLS. MY PENIS HAS GIVEN YOU UP. NOW IT PENETRATES MEN'S BEHINDS. GOODBYE, WONDROUS FEMININITY!

I HAVE BUGGERED MEN!

DEFECATOR, MAY EVERYTHING TURN OUT OKAY SO THAT YOU CAN LEAVE THIS PLACE

LESBIANUS, YOU DEFECATE AND YOU WRITE HELLO, EVERYONE!

RESTITUTUS SAYS, RESTITUTA TAKE OFF YOUR TUNIC, PLEASE, AND SHOW US YOUR HAIRY PRIVATES

THEOPHILUS, DO NOT PERFORM ORAL SEX ON GIRLS AGAINST THE CITY WALL LIKE A DOG

APOLLINARIS, THE DOCTOR OF THE EMPEROR TITVS, DEFECATED WELL HERE

FLORONIUS, PRIVILEGED SOLDIER OF THE 7TH LEGION, WAS HERE. THE WOMEN DID NOT KNOW OF HIS PRESENCE. ONLY SIX WOMEN CAME TO KNOW, TOO FEW FOR SUCH A STALLION

PHILEROS IS A EVNVCH!

I SCREWED A LOT OF GIRLS HERE

Aim! Fire!
. . . .

Fatboy Slim
. . . .

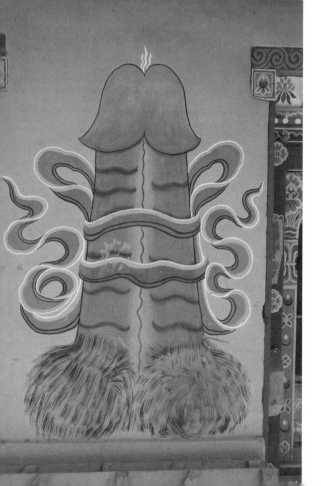

Aim high

· ·

In the West, the drawing of a spurting cock and balls is normally a hurried activity with the resulting artwork simple and crude. But perhaps we should be aiming higher – we could certainly learn a thing or two from the humble peasants of Bhutan who are the masters of phallic art. They proudly paint the sides of their houses with elaborately decorated, ejaculating, giant cocks, which often sit merrily atop a neatly coiffured ball sack.

Doodle dick

Take the weight off your gigantic . . .

Penis Museum

• •

'The foundation was laid in 1974 when I was given a pizzle or a bull's penis,' writes retired teacher Sigurður Hjartarson about the beginnings of his extraordinary collection of animal dongs. He now owns 280 specimens from ninety-three different species (including man), which are on display in the Icelandic Phallological Museum in Reykjavik. And it wouldn't be a museum without a shop, which stocks the usual array of T-shirts, key rings and ball scratchers.

Sigurður has now passed over curatorial duties to his son Hjörtur Gísli Sigurðsson, who – the website claims – 'is expected to set the standard for phallology worldwide.'

Earful
· · · · · · · · · · · ·

Baroque cock

· ·

Restoration experts in Valencia recently got a surprise when repairing a baroque vault in the cathedral – a hole in the ceiling unveiled a hidden fresco of angels. It had been painted in the fifteenth century by Paolo da San Leocadio, and was covered up in 1674 after water damage.

Even more surprising, though, was the graffiti they found – a cock and balls in one of the angel's wings. Not only that, but the seventeenth-century workmen had also flicked bits of soggy plaster onto the angels' mouths and eyes.

'They are exactly the same as you would find today in public toilets,' said the head of Valencia's Conservation Institute, Carmen Pérez.

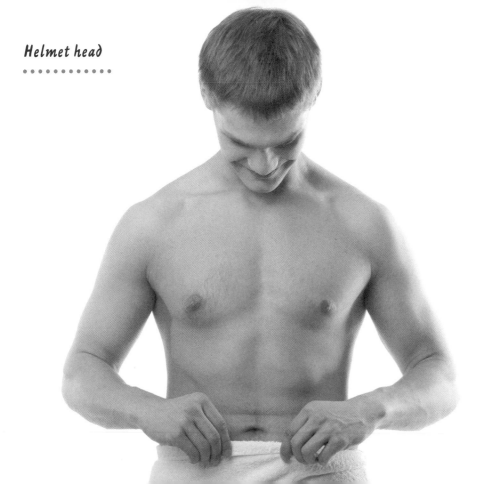

Helmet head
· · · · · · · · · · · ·

I'm too sexy for this shirt

Stick up

Nether regions

· ·

Everyone knows about the wonderfully named towns of Fucking in Austria and Dildo in Newfoundland but which of the following list are real place names and which have been made up?

1	Pratts Bottom	10	Tosside
2	Penistone	11	Bell End
3	Semen	12	Hairybumpton
4	Wetwang	13	Cockermouth
5	Lower Swell	14	Wankdorf
6	Shaven Snatch	15	Vibrator
7	Cockpocket	16	Balsak-in-the-Mouth
8	Bitchfield		
9	Comespital		

Just my type

You've been framed
. . . .

Classical education

What about Little Elvis?

Dave Lee Roth, lead singer of Van Halen, recently claimed that when the band go on tour he takes out an insurance policy with Lloyds of London for his penis, aka Little Elvis.

When asked by *The Huffington Post* whether he insured his whole body when on the road the poodle rocker replied, 'It wasn't my body, it was Little Elvis ... Before we were leaving they said, "We'll have to insure guitarist Eddie Van Halen's fingers, because he's going to be using those a lot on the road, and drummer Alex Van Halen's elbows, we're going to have to insure those because he's going to be using them a lot." And I said, "What about Little Elvis? We're going to be using him a lot."'

Spray paint

BA (Hons) Cockmuncher University

Cockhead

Coming to the top

More cock than balls

In his seminal 2009 work *Busty, Slag and Nob End*, Russell Ash conducted a survey of rude surnames by studying census and voter lists dating as far back as 1790. He was able to conclude that Cock was a far more popular surname than Balls – although both of these were less commonly found than Beaver. Ash also noted that research by Professor Richard Webber of King's College London had found that in the period between 1881 and 2008 the number of people called Cock had shrunk by seventy-five per cent, while Balls had dropped by over fifty per cent.

The top twenty were:

1	Beaver	11	Fucker
2	Cock	12	Knob
3	Balls	13	Bollock
4	Fanny	14	Boob
5	Boner	15	Sucker
6	Bonk	16	Wanker
7	Bastard	17	Cum
8	Minge	18	Prick
9	Wank	19	Bum
10	Nipple	20	Bugger

Cock-a-doodle

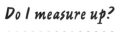

Do I measure up?

Hard times
. . . .

Eyeful tower

The great Greek tiddler mystery

Why are men in ancient Greek statues always naked? Well, their daily lives were conducted in clothes, but sports were played in the buff – the word gymnasium comes from the ancient Greek word *gymnós*, meaning naked – and lots of the statues depict men undertaking athletic exercise.

What is less clear is why all of them have such tiny cocks. Much academic debate has been centred on this question but no one seems to have an answer. Did the Greeks believe small cocks were more aesthetically pleasing, or did all that thinking help grow their brains but shrink their willies?

Jump for joy
· · · · · · · · · · · ·

Tick my box

A massive package
· · · · · · · · · · · · · · · ·

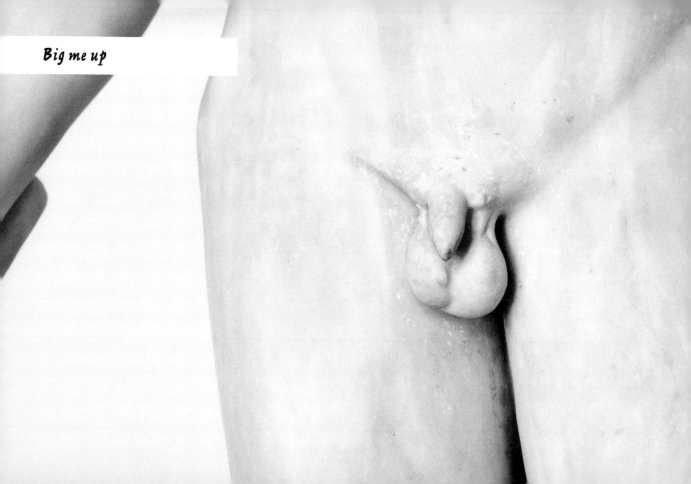

Big me up

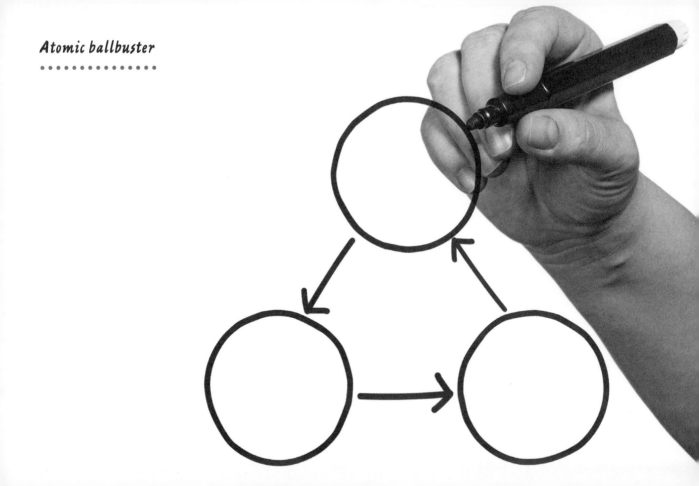

Yes, it's edible
. . . .

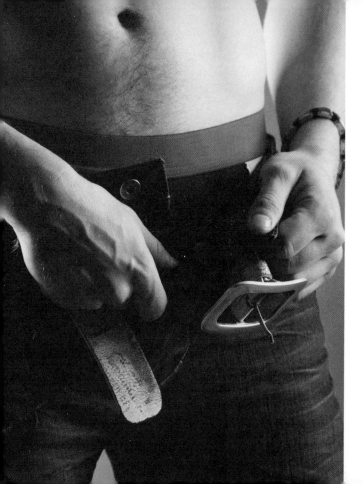

Zip it up

. . . .

Had Whitcomb L. Judson, inventor of the zipper, known that his creation was going to lead to an average of two thousand horrific penis injuries every year then perhaps he would have spent far less time developing his 'clasp locker'.

A recent paper in the journal *BJU International* showed that 17,616 people went to hospital with their tackle painfully stuck in their trousers between 2002 and 2010. A team from the University of California explained the stats further: 'The penis was almost always the only genital organ involved. Among adults, zips were the most frequent cause of penile injuries.'

Perhaps it's safer to let it all hang out.

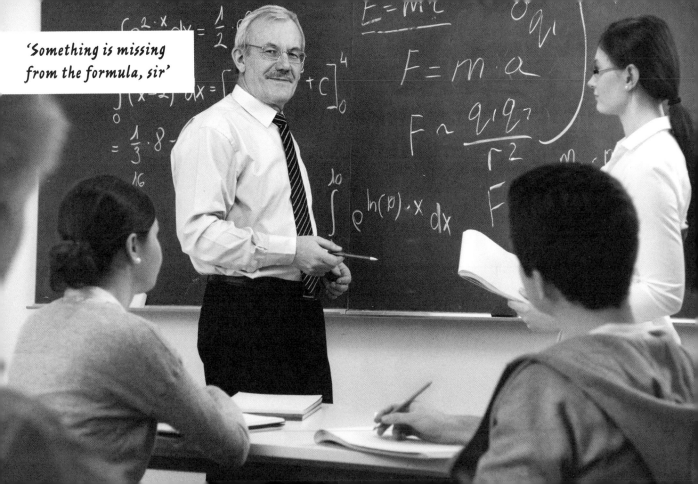

'Something is missing from the formula, sir'

Showerhead

· · · · · · · · · · · ·

Surprise, surprise
· · · · · · · · · · · · · · ·

By royal appointment

What's that noise?

· ·

The loudest creatures on earth, relative to size, are *Micronecta scholtzi*, a European species of tiny water boatman. They achieve levels of noise up to ninety-nine decibels, equivalent to the noise of a passing train, through a process known as 'stridulation', which is a fancy name for rubbing your penis against your arse.

The louder the noise the little boatmen make, the more likely they are to attract a mate. The reverse is true in humans: when the male rubs his penis, the female tends to run a mile.

Another insect, the pyrallid moth, can produce ultrasonic signals with its tiny nether regions. Although how it makes the noise continues to baffle scientists.

Skull and crossboner

Something's missing

Twin towers
. . . .

Pissing contest

. . . .

Standing opposite each other outside the Franz Kafka Museum in Prague are two full-size statues of men urinating. Although the world is full of pissing statues, these are a little bit special – while the penis moves up and down, the stream of water writes out quotes from famous Prague residents.

The. artist David Černý's other great works include a thirty-foot high statue with a ladder leading to its backside. If you climb the ladder you can put your head inside the statue's anus and watch a short movie of two old men feeding each other to Queen's 'We Are The Champions'.

Ball bag
· · · · · · · · · ·

Shrunk in the wash

· · · · · · · · · · · · · · · · ·

Back to back

Keep off the grass

Take a load of that

· ·

In May 2008, *Lonesome Cowboy* – a six-feet-high anime-inspired sculpture by the Japanese artist Takashi Murakami – came up for auction at Sotheby's. It was bought by an anonymous bidder for $13.5 million.

It is not surprising that the purchaser wanted to remain anonymous, as who would want to own up to spending that amount of cash on a life-size sculpture of a masturbating boy shooting a semen lasso out of his bell end?

Growing old disgracefully

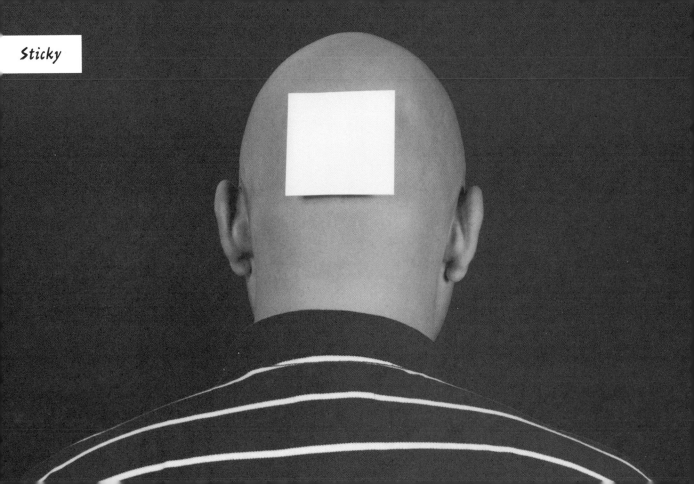

Touch your toes

· · · · · · · · · · · · · · · ·

Reach for the sky
• • • • • • • • • • • • • • • •

Penis park

· ·

On the east coast of Korea is a very grown-up tourist attraction: Haesindang Park (Penis Park) which contains over sixty giant wooden cocks.

Legend has it that when a local virgin was swept out to sea a curse was placed on the village fishing boats. But one day a local man happened to be masturbating into the sea (as you do) and miraculously the fishermen began catching fish again. It was felt, rather than get the local men to wank into the sea, the same effect could be achieved by carving these giant phallic symbols.

Male visitors to the park are respectfully asked to unbutton their flies and walk around with their penises hanging out for the duration of their stay.

Put it away, Santa

That's gotta hurt
· · · · · · · · · · · · · · ·

DIY

KITCHEN

Penis theft

· ·

'It's real. Just yesterday here, there was a man who was a victim. We saw. What was left was tiny,' said twenty-nine-year-old Alain Kalala to a Reuters reporter in Kinshasa, Congo back in 2008.

He wasn't the only victim; a wave of penis thefts was sweeping the capital. Fourteen people claimed that witch doctors had either removed their penises completely or reduced them to an embarrassing stub.

The police decided to arrest both the sorcerers and the victims in an attempt to avoid a repeat of the violence that accompanied a penis panic ten years earlier, when twelve cock thieves were murdered by mobs of angry citizens.

Mouthful

My name is . . .

King Dong

Masked member
· · · · · · · · · · · · · · ·

Tittle Cock bridge

was opened on 27th June 2008 by

Councillor Denise Jeffery

puty Leader of Wakefield Council and Cabin

lember for Regeneration, Culture and Sport,

and Councillor Mark Burns Williamson

Tittle my cock

In 2010, a group of vociferous over-sixties won a campaign to have a newly installed plaque removed from a bridge in Yorkshire.

Margaret from the Voice of the Elderly explained to a local paper, 'The old plaque was wrong, it had the wrong name on and we were offended by it. It was important to keep the name rather than having a new one just because someone decided it sounded a bit better.'

The bridge had been known for generations as Tickle Cock bridge but the council wanted to change the name to the more politically correct 'Tittle Cott'. Thankfully, the old folks won the day and Tickle Cock it remains.

Sandy balls

Madame Palm

Aim well
· · · · · · · · ·

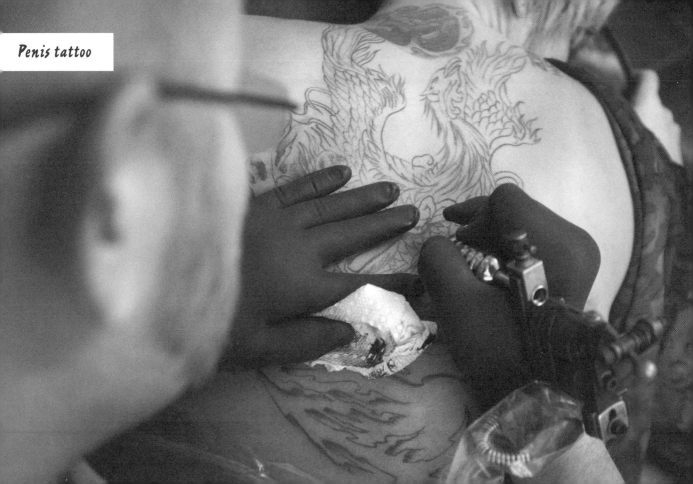

Penis tattoo

Hello, sailor

What a beautiful view

Rocket launcher

Shot your bolt

. . . .

In 2008, a Croatian biker was left wishing he had waited until the next service station rather than pissed at the side of the road when his pecker was hit by lightning and he was knocked unconscious.

Ante Djindjic, from Zagreb, said, 'I don't remember what happened. One minute I was taking a leak and the next thing I knew I was in hospital. Doctors said the lightning went through my body and, because I was wearing rubber boots, it earthed itself through my penis. Thankfully, the doctors said that there would be no lasting effects, and my penis will function normally eventually.'

I think the key word in that quote is 'eventually'.

Shrivel

Get wood

Peel it back

Tattooed member

Spit it out

· ·

The Latin botanical name is *Senecio jacobaea* and it is part of the Compositae family that also includes asters and sunflowers. It grows up to a metre high, has long, jagged leaves and small yellow flowers that look a bit like daisies. It is, of course, more commonly known as Stinking Willie.

Next time you are on a boring family walk you can point across the field and say completely seriously to your girlfriend's mum, 'Is that a Stinking Willie over there?' And, knowing that the plant is poisonous to cattle, it wouldn't be too rude to say, 'I hope that cow doesn't put the Stinking Willie in her mouth. She needs to spit it out. You should never swallow a Stinking Willie.'

It's a whopper
. . . .

I'm still standing

Big board

Floater

Grinder man

In 2010, a fire crew were called to Southampton Hospital, UK to help free a man's penis that had got stuck 'accidently' in a steel pipe.

The man had arrived that morning, carefully clutching the pipe, and was unwilling to offer an explanation as to how the 'accident' had occurred. The firemen used a large metal grinder to cut through the steel, later explaining that a delicate operation was made worse because the man's penis was erect due to a restriction of blood flow (or the fact that he was a total pervert?).

Thankfully, the operation was a success, although his manhood was left bruised – though not as much as his pride.

I can't keep it down

Mine's bigger than yours
· ·

On a plate

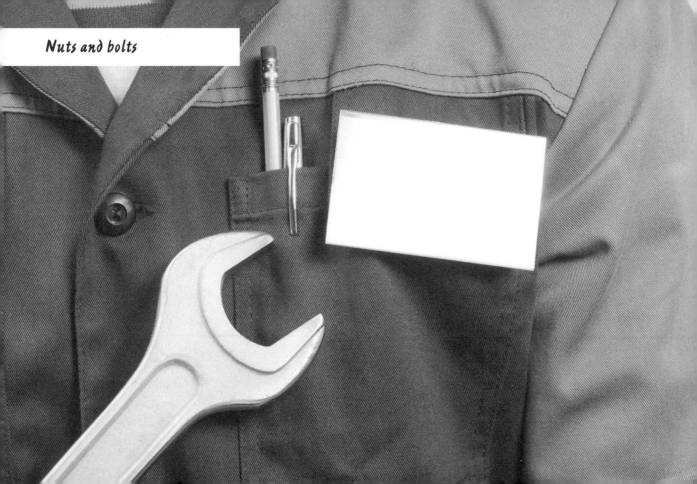

Nuts and bolts

A couple of pointers

Tit fountain

The official website of Nuremberg features this harrowingly dull description of its sixteenth-century fountain, created by Benedikt Wurzelbau in 1589:

> Six allegories of the three theological and the three cardinal virtues with their attributes are placed on a round platform: Faith with a cross and a chalice, Love with two children, Hope with an anchor, Courage with a lion, Moderation with a jug, and Patience with a lamb ... The seventh virtue, Justice, stands on the top of the pillar with blindfolded eyes, a sword and a crane as a symbol of alertness.

Oh yes and water shoots out of their tits – you somehow forgot to mention that.

Shock and awe

· · · · · · · · · · · · · ·

Rain on me
· · · · · · · · · · ·

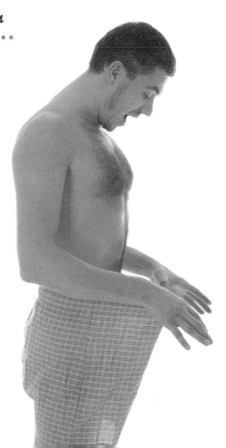

Work it, baby

· · · · · · · · · · · · ·

Laced with alcohol

· ·

An unusual medical case from 1930s Australia was reported in the *Fortean Times*. A middle-aged labourer complained to his doctor that going for a pee had become unbearably painful. Surgeons operated and found the cause of his discomfort – a bootlace in the bladder.

The labourer said the pain began the day after a prolonged drinking session with his workmates about which he could remember little. It was concluded that at some point in the evening his so-called friends must have inserted the bootlace down his penis. He was advised in future to be more careful about the company he kept.

Beachballs

Obst
Brot
Milch
Wein
Nudeln
Zucker

Cheerleader

Get a load of this

Lit up

One we made earlier . . .